Jed's Big Adventure

The Shark Guardian Series Book Two

written and illustrated by
Gail Clarke

This book is for shark guardians everywhere and especially for

.... (your name)

Some time ago you may have read
Of Jed, the scalloped hammerhead.
Where is he now this special shark?
He's in the mangroves, cool and dark.

These shallow waters are his home
Where young Jed is free to roam
Amongst the tangled trees that grow,
Their leaves above, their roots below.

Now that several months have passed,
Jed the shark is growing fast.
He must rely on all his senses —
They are his number one defences.

His hearing, sight and sense of smell
Have all developed very well.
They help to keep him safe from dangers
Like larger sharks and hungry strangers.

Jed's smart, he's quick, he knows the way
To search for food and hunt his prey.
Sardines, mackerel, little fish,
All make a most delicious dish.
And squid is quite a special treat
For a growing hammerhead to eat.

But food in the mangroves cannot give
The nourishment Jed needs to live;
To help him grow and make him stronger
He can't remain here for much longer.
It's time to find a hunting ground
Where more nutritious prey is found;
He has to leave but doesn't know
In which direction he should go.

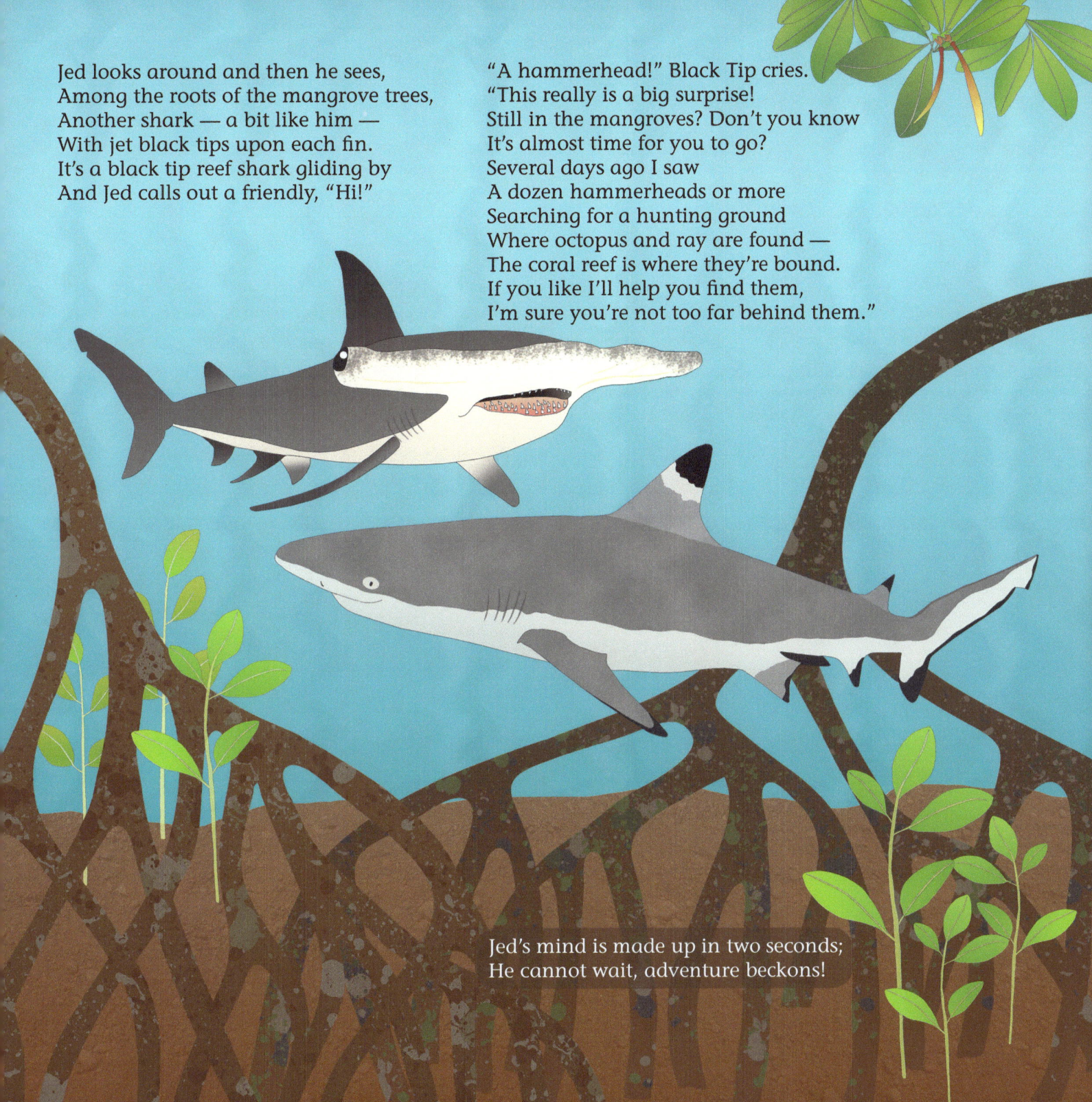

Jed looks around and then he sees,
Among the roots of the mangrove trees,
Another shark — a bit like him —
With jet black tips upon each fin.
It's a black tip reef shark gliding by
And Jed calls out a friendly, "Hi!"

"A hammerhead!" Black Tip cries.
"This really is a big surprise!
Still in the mangroves? Don't you know
It's almost time for you to go?
Several days ago I saw
A dozen hammerheads or more
Searching for a hunting ground
Where octopus and ray are found —
The coral reef is where they're bound.
If you like I'll help you find them,
I'm sure you're not too far behind them."

Jed's mind is made up in two seconds;
He cannot wait, adventure beckons!

The new friends set off side by side
With Black Tip acting as a guide.

They haven't gone too far before
They see strange things on the ocean floor.
Where the coral should be growing
Piles of junk are overflowing:
Cans and bottles, old tyres too,
Used batteries, phones and quite a few
Bits of glass and broken dishes,
Plastic bags like jellyfishes,
Fishing nets — which could drown them —
Trash and plastic all around them,
Thrown away without a care
For any creature living there.

Black Tip sighs, "Thoughtless humans are the ones!
They dump these countless millions of tons
Of things they don't want any more
To fall as trash to the ocean floor.
Tides and currents then bring them here,
And the piles get bigger every year."

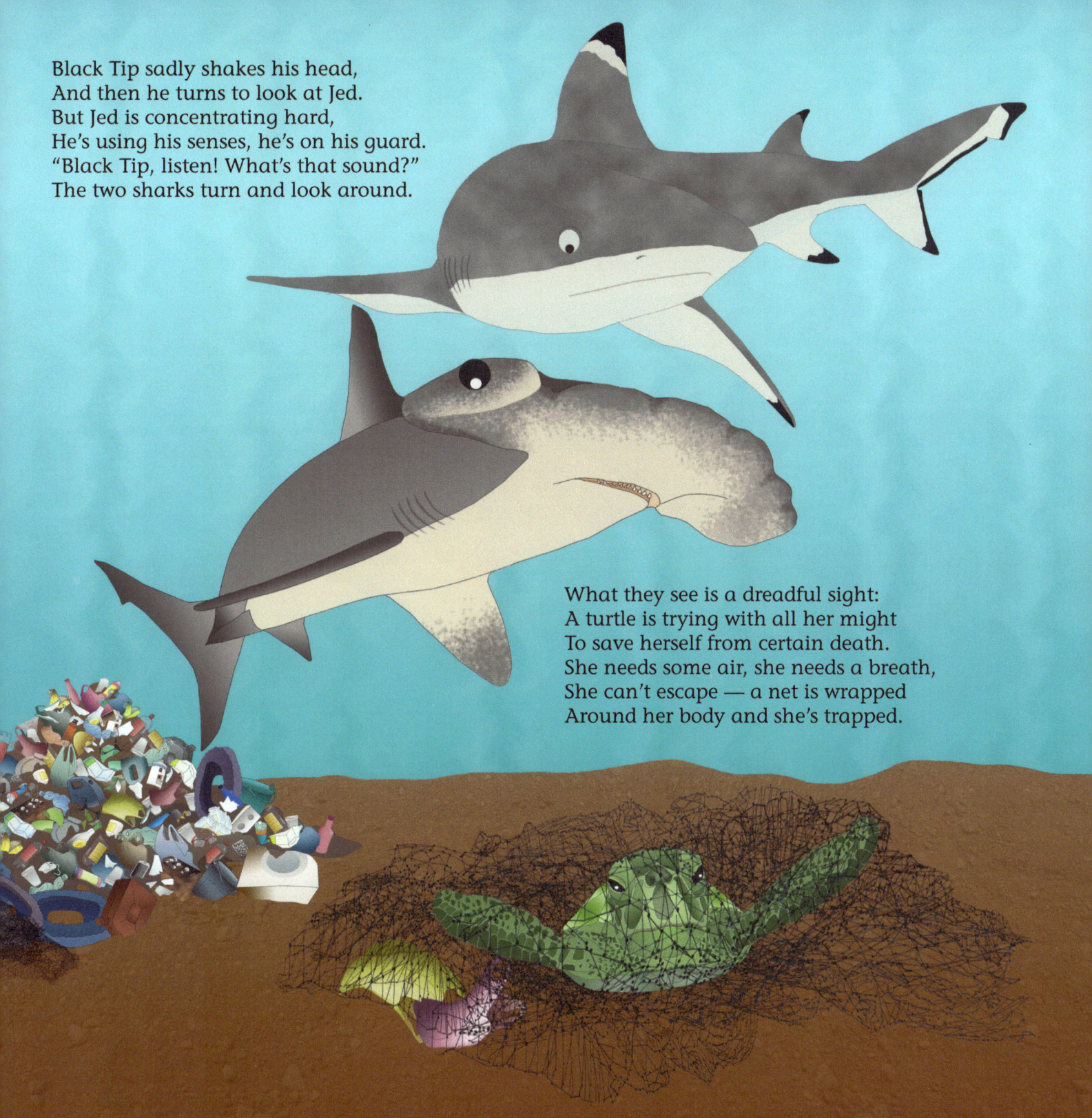

Black Tip sadly shakes his head,
And then he turns to look at Jed.
But Jed is concentrating hard,
He's using his senses, he's on his guard.
"Black Tip, listen! What's that sound?"
The two sharks turn and look around.

What they see is a dreadful sight:
A turtle is trying with all her might
To save herself from certain death.
She needs some air, she needs a breath,
She can't escape — a net is wrapped
Around her body and she's trapped.

"Come on!" Jed calls. "Black Tip, make haste,
There isn't any time to waste!
We have to set her free right now,
We have the tools and I know how.
Our teeth are sharp enough to cut
This net of nylon fishing gut.
Turtle, stay still! Be brave and strong!
This job won't take us very long."

The two friends work with lightning speed
And very quickly she is freed.

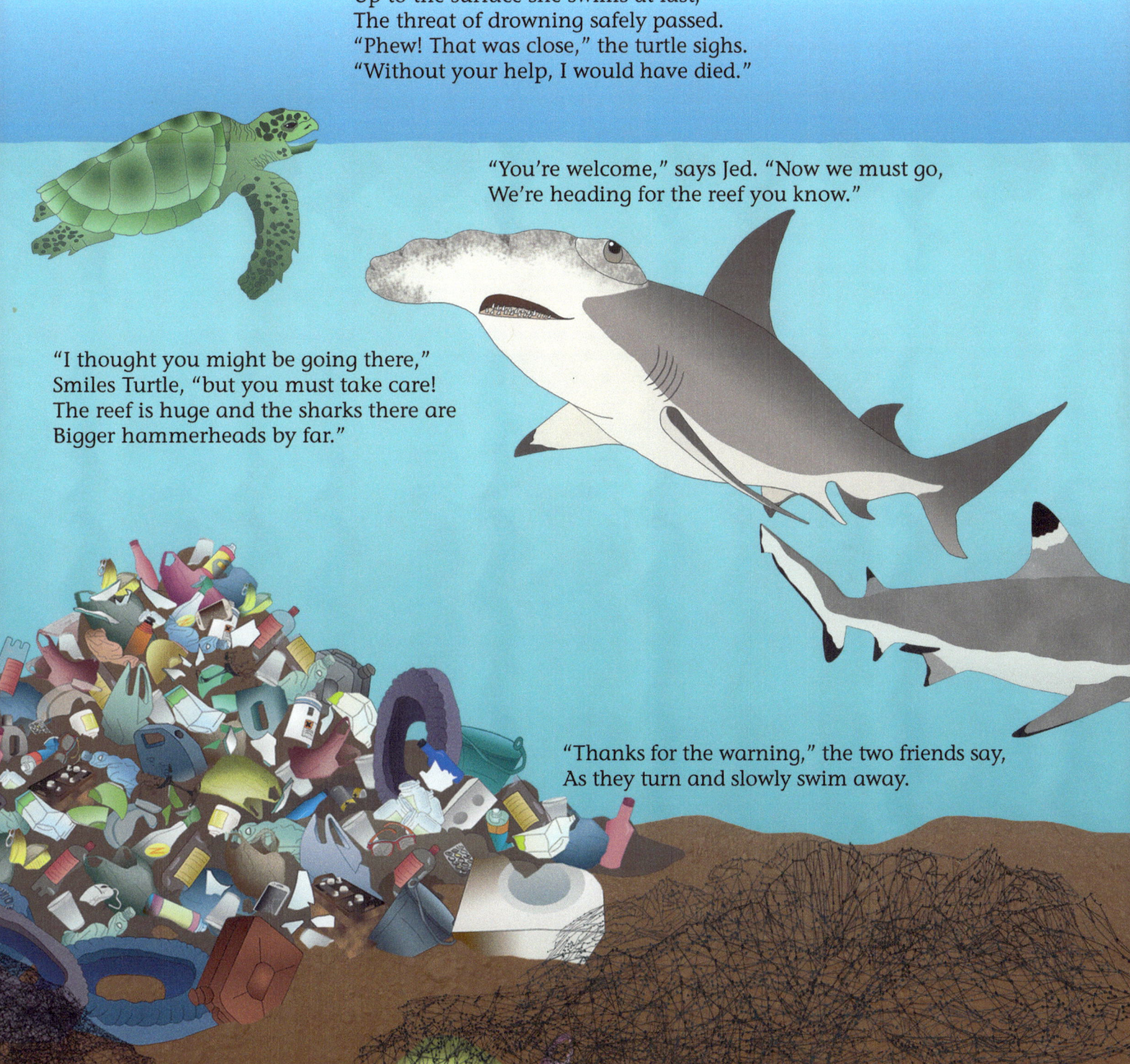

Up to the surface she swims at last,
The threat of drowning safely passed.
"Phew! That was close," the turtle sighs.
"Without your help, I would have died."

"You're welcome," says Jed. "Now we must go,
We're heading for the reef you know."

"I thought you might be going there,"
Smiles Turtle, "but you must take care!
The reef is huge and the sharks there are
Bigger hammerheads by far."

"Thanks for the warning," the two friends say,
As they turn and slowly swim away.

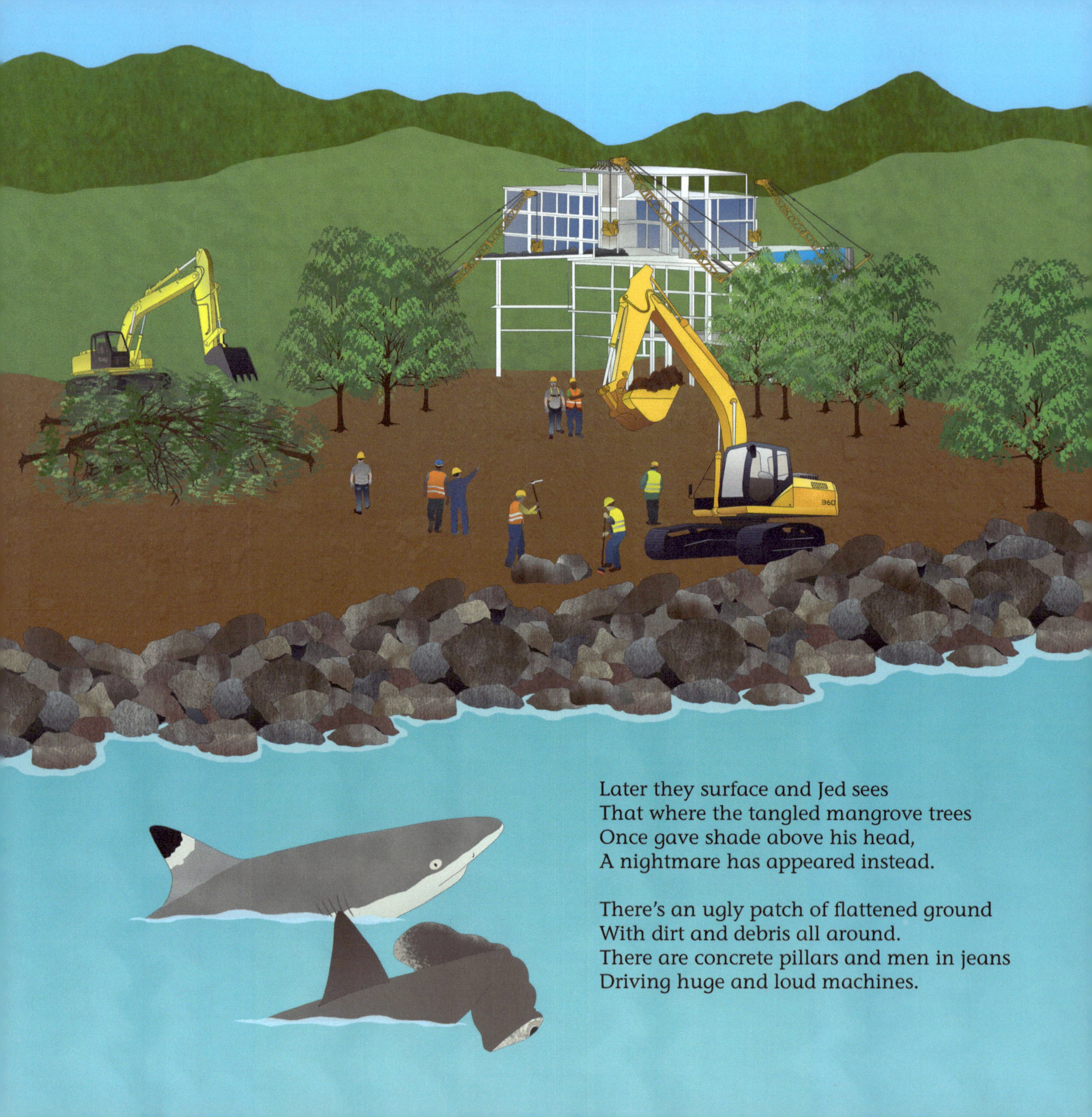

Later they surface and Jed sees
That where the tangled mangrove trees
Once gave shade above his head,
A nightmare has appeared instead.

There's an ugly patch of flattened ground
With dirt and debris all around.
There are concrete pillars and men in jeans
Driving huge and loud machines.

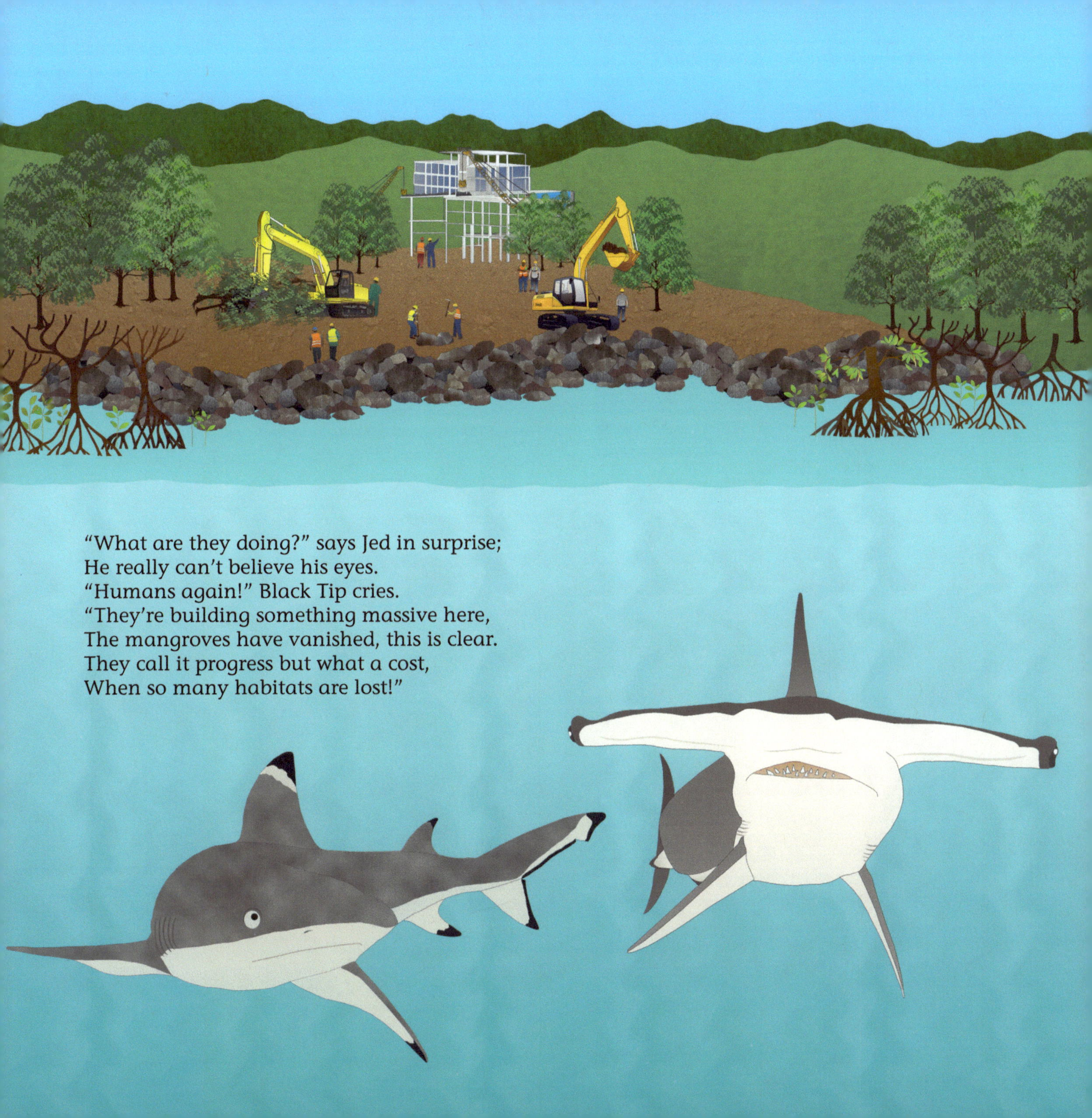

"What are they doing?" says Jed in surprise;
He really can't believe his eyes.
"Humans again!" Black Tip cries.
"They're building something massive here,
The mangroves have vanished, this is clear.
They call it progress but what a cost,
When so many habitats are lost!"

They leave the awful place and then
Swim towards the reef again.
As they journey on they pass
A waving patch of green sea grass.

"Soon," says Black Tip, "you will be
Heading for the open sea."
"I will, my old friend," Jed replies,
With shaky voice and shining eyes.
"I've heard it's scary but exciting,
Dangerous, yet so inviting."

"We've reached the shallow reef my friend,
My journey's almost at its end,"
Says Black Tip. "But before I go
Perhaps you'd like to say hello
To a very curious shark I know."

Suddenly, from the coral bed,
Up pops a very stripy head,
A body that's both white and black
With a long and very bendy back.
He's small, he's very young, not more
Than three months old, or maybe four.
The shoals of bright fish swimming near
Are terrified of him it's clear,
And in an instant disappear.

"I'm Zebra Shark," their friend explains,
"But little fish have little brains!
They always make the same mistake
And think that I'm a striped sea snake.
My stripes are similar it's true
But really, I'm a shark like you."

"And if you think that this sounds strange,
Later on my colours change.
While I'm young these stripes are clear,
But as I grow they'll disappear.
I'll turn light brown with spots instead
That cover me from tail to head."

"A zebra shark with SPOTS, dear me!"
Chuckles Jed. "How can this be?
Zebras have STRIPES — you must be joking!"
He laughs so hard he's almost choking.

"I know it's weird," the young shark cries,
"But I'm a master of disguise."

As the three approach the deeper reef,
Jed cries out in disbelief,
"Look ahead there — can you see
A group of hammerheads like me?
There must be twenty sharks or more,
It's the group that we've been searching for.
Hurry, you two, let's go and greet them,
I can't wait for us to meet them."

Black Tip answers with a sigh,
"It's time for us to say goodbye.
Ahead lies your new hunting ground,
But the two of us must turn around
And go back to the homes we know
In the shallows, where the mangroves grow."

"Goodbye! Good luck!" the three friends say.
"Perhaps we'll meet again some day."
Then Black Tip and Zebra Shark swim away.

Jed is nervous but excited,
He wonders if he'll be invited.
Is this where his future lies
Until he grows to adult size?

Suddenly, he hears them call,
"Hi there! Come and join us all!"

Out looking for food the very next day,
The sharks see a shoal of bluespotted ray.

The rays are green with bright blue spots.
How many are there? Lots and lots!
Their outspread fins are more like wings;
Their tails have very poisonous stings.
And the holes above each yellow eye
Are their nostrils — the rays' oxygen supply.
Rays don't have teeth, it's strange but true,
So when eating their food, what do they do?
There are crushers under each ray's head
That they use to squash their prey instead.

The feeding rays are unaware
That a school of hungry sharks is there.
But the sharks are ready for some fun,
So they challenge Jed to capture one.
Jed looks at the rays and feels a thrill;
It's time to test his hunting skill.

Down Jed dives to the ocean floor,
He's never hunted ray before.
As he gets closer, many hide
And others scatter far and wide.
In seconds, they all disappear,
There's not a single ray left here.
"Don't be upset," the others say,
"You need to practise trapping ray.
You have to use your hammerhead
To pin them down on the ocean bed."

The sharks swim off without further fuss,
"We're heading to the drop-off, come with us.
The seabed there is extremely steep
And the ocean dark and very deep."

Suddenly, Jed hears a sound.
He turns and as he looks around
A moray eel is slowly sliding
From a cave where he is hiding.

"Heading for the drop, I see,
Well, first you have to get past me!
My name is Scarface and I'm a breed
That's very dangerous indeed.
I may look like a harmless snake
But I'm an eel, make no mistake!
My mouth is large, my teeth are too,
They're large enough to dine on you!"

"I got this scar from fishing hooks.
They spoiled my young and handsome looks.
This is why, you must agree,
Everyone is scared of me."

Jed looks at the creature in dismay
And wonders if there is a way
To get beyond this fearsome foe,
To safer waters far below.

"Now listen, Scarface," answers Jed,
"I'm a scalloped hammerhead.
I'm brave, I'm strong, I'm clever too,
And I am not afraid of YOU!"

When Scarface chuckles, Jed's confused —
Why is the creature so amused?
The moray laughs, "You've passed the test,
And now I wish you all the best.
I wanted you to be quite sure
That you are really ready for
Everything that lies ahead.
Goodbye! Good luck! Safe journey, Jed!"

After passing Scarface, Jed sees the drop;
It almost makes his young heart stop.
How deep is it? He's very sure
It's miles down to the ocean floor.

Jed swims faster, it's time to go,
He plunges to the depths below…

SHARK FACTS

The head of a hammerhead shark is called its cephalofoil. It uses this to pin rays onto the sea floor and feed on them. Hammerheads have widely set eyes that give them almost 360 degree vision.

Like all sharks, hammerheads have tiny pores called ampullae of Lorenzini. These are so sensitive that sharks can even detect the heartbeat of prey that is hiding deep below them under the sand.

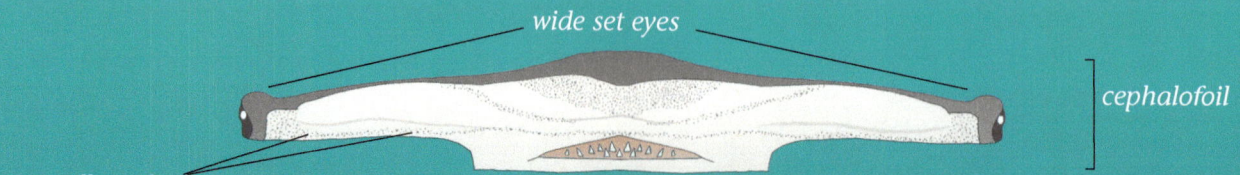

wide set eyes

cephalofoil

Ampullae of Lorenzini — tiny pores on the head that are sensitive to electrical impulses from other creatures

Hammerheads, blue sharks, bull sharks and lemon sharks are some of the types that are born fully developed. They are called viviparous. Other sharks that develop in egg form are called oviparous.

viviparous sharks are born fully developed

oviparous sharks develop in an egg which will hatch

Although sharks' ears are very small, they are far more sensitive than human ears. A shark can hear sounds from more than a kilometre away, such as the noise made by a struggling fish.

ear

ear

Like fingerprints in humans, the spots of an adult zebra shark are unique.

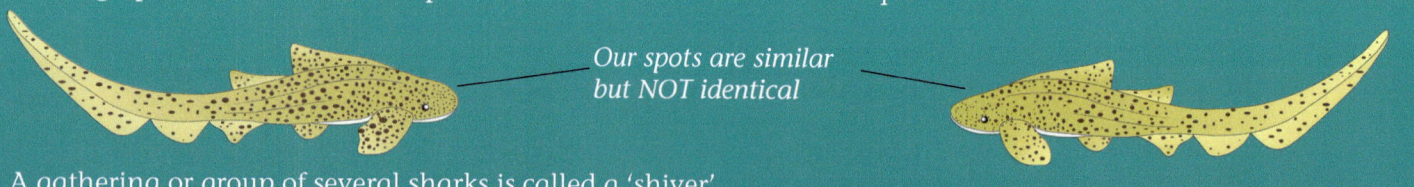

Our spots are similar but NOT identical

A gathering or group of several sharks is called a 'shiver'.

a shiver of sharks

mangroves

Mangroves provide an important nursery ground for many juvenile sharks and other marine species.

PROBLEMS FACING OUR OCEANS

By the year 2050 there could be more plastic in our oceans than plankton, threatening the survival of large plankton–feeding sharks and mammals.

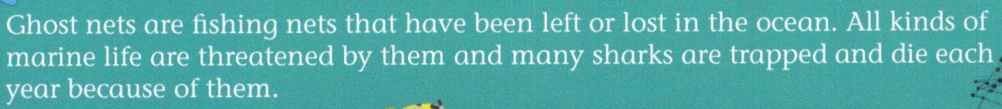

Ghost nets are fishing nets that have been left or lost in the ocean. All kinds of marine life are threatened by them and many sharks are trapped and die each year because of them.

JOIN DON AND IZZY

Be a Shark Guardian with Don and Izzy by following these four steps to protect sharks:

***DO NOT** buy any shark-related products such as shark teeth or jaws as souvenirs.

***DO NOT** eat shark meat or shark fin soup! Sharks die when their fins are cut off.

***AVOID** using plastic straws, bags, drinks bottles and cutlery: **REDUCE, REUSE, RECYCLE!**

***DO** participate in beach clean ups and get your friends involved too.

JED'S CHALLENGE

There are three types of plankton-feeding sharks in the world. Can you name them?

Visit our website for other downloadable tools and resources: *www.sharkguardian.org*

Children's shark artwork from schools around the world.

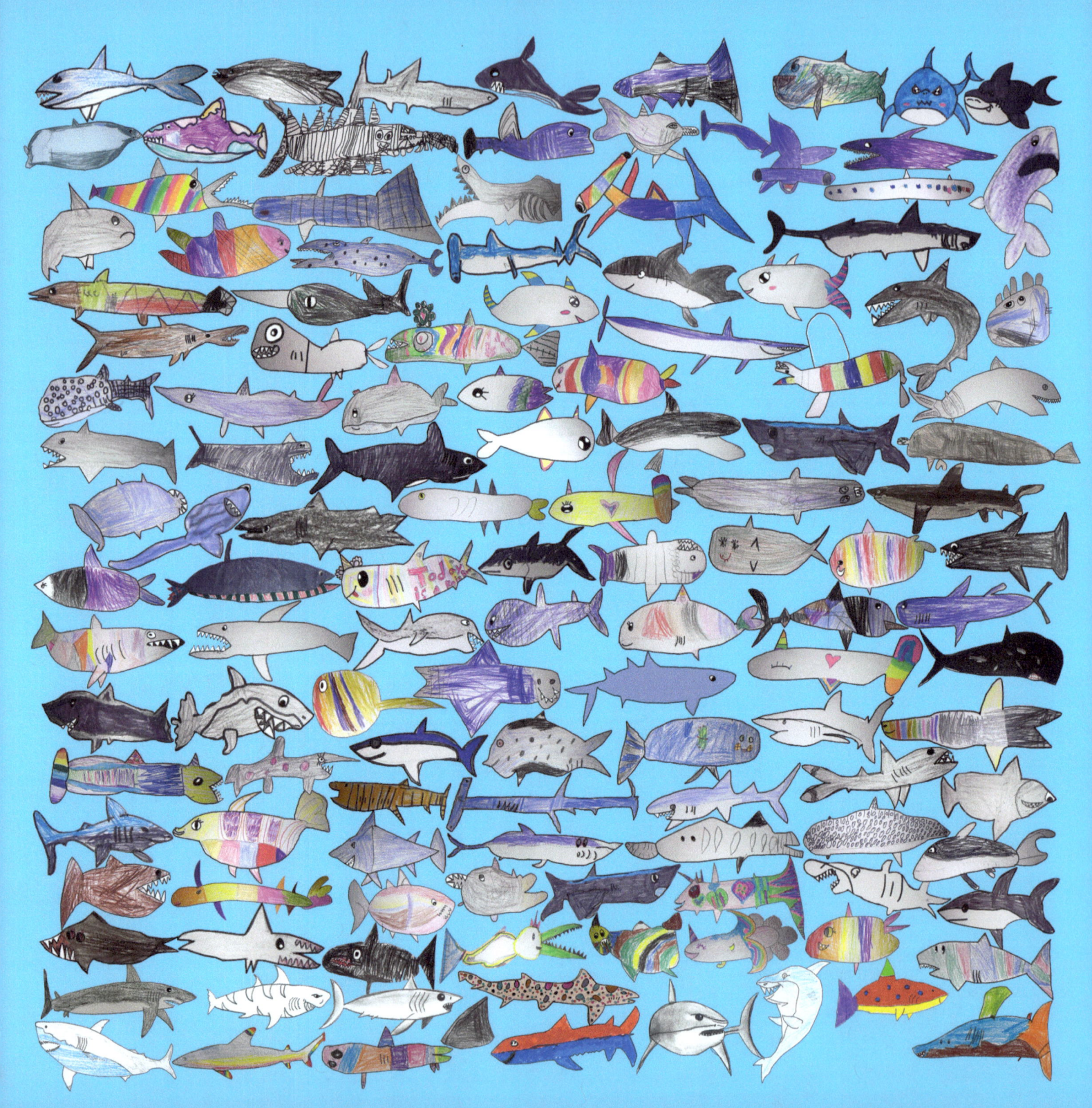

A Note from Shark Guardian charity directors Brendon Sing and Liz Ward-Sing

Dear Parents, Teachers and Shark Guardians,

We are super-excited to work once more with Gail Clarke and bring you Book Two in the Shark Guardian series. We hope you enjoy learning more about hammerheads — always a firm favourite amongst children when we visit schools around the world!

Since we released our first book 'Sharks Our Ocean Guardians', there has been a huge focus worldwide on the bigger challenges facing sharks and other marine creatures. We hope that by including issues such as coastal development, trash and pollution in Jed's adventures, we can all work together to help sharks and our oceans in general.

A huge thanks to Gail for the enormous amount of work she has put into this book. We hope you enjoy it as much as we do — please keep sharing our important messages from the book and learn more about sharks on our website *www.sharkguardian.org*. As Shark Guardians around the world, we can work together to help secure the future of this most important species.

We hope to see you in person on one of our school or community tours one day!
Best wishes,

Liz, Brendon and the Shark Guardian Team

Find out more about Liz, Brendon, Shark Guardian, sharks and ocean conservation at *www.sharkguardian.org*

A note from children's author, illustrator and storyteller Gail Clarke

Hi,

I hope you enjoyed 'Jed's Big Adventure' and meeting his new friends. I certainly enjoyed writing and illustrating the book. I learned a lot about sharks and about looking after the ocean and all its creatures along the way. Did you learn something too?

There will be a third book in the series in which you can follow Jed's shark guardian deeds as he explores the deeper ocean, encounters lots of exciting creatures and faces new challenges. His mission is to help keep sharks and all marine life safe and our oceans clean and healthy.

I have written and illustrated seven other books about animals which I have presented to more than thirty-five thousand children around the world. If I haven't already met you or visited your school, I hope to do so one day! I know that many of you are planet guardians and understand how important it is to look after our precious planet and all its species. Keep up the good work! By working together, we can make a real difference.

You can find out more about my books, about writing and illustrating, and about my school visits by looking at my website: *www.gailclarkeauthor.com*

Copyright © 2019 Gail Clarke,
Original text: Gail Clarke, illustrations: Gail Clarke
ISBN 978-1-912406-31-9
All rights reserved
Published by Gupole Publications

Shark Guardian: www.sharkguardian.org
Gail Clarke: www.gailclarkeauthor.com

www.ingramcontent.com/pod-product-compliance
Lightning Source LLC
Chambersburg PA
CBHW042249100526
44587CB00002B/80